Not another...meeting!

Not another...meeting!

How to make meetings effective and enjoyable

John Cox

kevin mayhew

kevin
mayhew

First published in Great Britain in 2015 by Kevin Mayhew Ltd
Buxhall, Stowmarket, Suffolk IP14 3BW
Tel: +44 (0) 1449 737978 Fax: +44 (0) 1449 737834
E-mail: info@kevinmayhew.com

www.kevinmayhew.com

9 8 7 6 5 4 3 2 1 0

ISBN 978 1 84867 805 7
Catalogue No. 1501500

Cover design by Rob Mortonson
© Image used under licence from Shutterstock Inc.
Edited by Nicki Copeland
Typeset by Angela Selfe

Printed and bound in Great Britain

Contents

About the author

Having spent rather a long time at various universities including Cambridge, Oxford and the University College of Rhodesia and Nyasaland, John was ordained to a curacy in the diocese of Liverpool in 1968. He spent a second curacy in an inner-city ex-slum parish in Birmingham and became rector in the same parish. After a five-year period at Church House, Westminster where he was Senior Selection Secretary, helping to select ordinands, he was made Canon Treasurer at Southwark Cathedral and Diocesan Director of Ordinands and Post-ordination training.

Following four years as Vicar of Roehampton he moved to become Archdeacon of Sudbury in the Diocese of St Edmundsbury and Ipswich in 1995. When he retired in 2006 he was asked to be the part-time Diocesan Director of Education, a job he did for nearly four and a half years before retiring for a second time. It has been during these retirement years that John has been writing for Kevin Mayhew, in between being chair of governors at a primary academy, playing golf and enjoying river cruises.

For details of all John Cox's books, please visit our website: www.kevinmayhew.com

Introduction

I hate meetings. Well, actually that is not quite true. It's certain kinds of meetings I dislike. Over the years I've been to more than my fair share of meetings of all sorts, and a good many have been fine. It's not a particular type of meeting that gets my goat; it's the way meetings are run and the way members of the meeting behave (or don't behave) that cause the problem. And that can happen any time, anywhere.

While I may be rapidly becoming a grumpy old man, I don't believe I'm unique in having this view about meetings. You've probably experienced it yourself. The meeting began late and went on far too long. No one seemed to be clear about the purpose of the meeting. By the end people were agreeing to things just so they could get home or to the pub. Papers were tabled instead of being distributed before the meeting and a lot of time was wasted while people attempted to make sense of 12 pages of legal gobbledygook or financial statements with no one around the table having the knowledge or expertise to explain them. Most of the decisions seemed to have already been made, contributions were kept to a minimum while the chair rabbited on, and voting felt like applying a rubber stamp. When there was discussion, it was ill-tempered and resulted in decisions that simply preserved the status quo and the power of the 'inner' group. At some point it wasn't even clear whether or not a decision had been made. There was more animated discussion in the loo afterwards than there had been at the meeting. Two of the silent members made it known that they hadn't agreed with one of the decisions and they didn't mind who knew they had voted against it.

To summarise it in that way, of course, is an exaggeration. I don't suppose even a really bad meeting would have all those elements. But they are a fair representation of what makes for bad meetings and what makes people dislike meetings. And if the members are volunteers, too many meetings like that will make them leave – if they have any sense.

The majority of the meetings I have attended over the years have involved the church both at local, parish level and at diocesan level. As an archdeacon, meetings came with the territory. Not all of those meetings were particularly pleasant experiences. It would be nice to think that Christian people know both how to lead meetings and how to behave in meetings. It's not necessarily so.

My experience has been in the Church of England, so I have spoken to members of other denominations about how their meetings go. As you might expect, it's a mixed picture. But some are certainly better than others. None is perfect – not simply because all human activity is less than perfect, but also because the structures that establish and sustain meetings are themselves not perfect, at least not for every activity that meetings seek to achieve.

Meetings come in all sorts and sizes and have different purposes in mind. They will vary from a few people gathered around in a sitting room to a full church hall. Some meetings are called to conduct the everyday running of the organisation, others to plan a protest, some to organise a fundraising campaign, others to plan the Christmas Fayre. In general it's the committee type meeting I shall be concerned with, although there are occasional glances at others. Some points are general enough to apply to most types of meetings; some will necessarily be more specific.

Whatever the purpose, whatever the size, whatever the membership, if you are going to hold a meeting it needs to be effective. If it's not, people have every reason to grumble. To make a meeting effective everyone needs to be playing their part – in a positive way. So this isn't just a book for chairpersons; it is for anyone who attends meetings.

In this book I have set out to help both those who are responsible for meetings – chairs and officers – and those who attend meetings. I want to encourage them to think about what they are doing and seeking to achieve, and to help them find ways to improve. It's not rocket science, and I don't kid myself that I have discovered some novel guaranteed solution. But given the number of meetings a lot of people do attend, it would be good if more were effective and fewer people ended up saying, 'Not another . . . meeting.'

Frank If we have another meeting like that, I'm resigning. Do you see the time? The pub'll be shut if we don't hurry. It's ridiculous. Sid arrived late and then Peggy had to leave halfway through.

Charles I know. But the date did get changed at the last minute. And why did we spend all that time on the colour of the notepaper? You'd have thought last year's deficit was a lot more important, but that got rushed through.

Frank Have you seen the accounts? I didn't get my copy till yesterday. I ask you. What's the good of that! The way they set them out it takes me ages to work out what's what.

Charles You were lucky. Most papers seem to get tabled. That really annoys me. How are we supposed to deal with them properly like that? I've told the chair but he seems to take no notice. Just blames it on the secretary.

Frank He just does what he wants anyhow. The way he shut Jane up you'd think he didn't want us there. Well, if it goes on like this I won't be. Want a drink?

ONE

Membership

Most organisations have meetings to conduct some aspect of business. It is not usual for the whole membership of the organisation to be present, and therefore they are not 'members' of that meeting.

However, this is not universally true, and the meetings held by Quakers are a case in point. For Quakers, business meetings are actually meetings for worship where there is a prearranged agenda for discussion and decision. This is based on the concept that all meetings should be an act of worship and that all business decisions should be made in the context of discerning the guidance of the Holy Spirit within worship. All members have the right to be at the meeting and to speak, as led by the Spirit.

Attendance at a meeting may also be extended beyond members. For example, a local authority council meeting may be open to the public, but the public do not have members' rights in that they may not speak or vote.

Whatever the arrangement, it is clear that the membership of a meeting is a key element in the meeting's effectiveness.

People will sometimes be willing to complain in public about the way meetings are run: the length or lack of the agenda, the way minutes have been written, the failure to keep to time. Complaints about the people involved tend to be made more privately, away from the meeting itself.

Yet it is the members present at the meeting who have most influence upon what happens, for good or ill. How people behave in meetings depends on a range of complex and interacting factors, including:

- their personal agenda;
- their personality;
- their knowledge, experience and expertise;
- their relationships;
- their roles and responsibilities and how well they understand these;
- the number of members in the group;
- how the members came to be included in the meeting;
- whether they are volunteers or attending in a paid capacity.

Let's work back through these.

Members

a. Volunteers

The majority of local church meetings involve volunteers. Apart from the minister, there may be no one who is paid by the church. The same will be true of school governors where all are volunteers apart from the head teacher and possibly the clerk to the governors. Contrast this with a meeting of local authority officials, senior managers in a factory or members of a legal practice where all are present because they are paid to be. Even that is not always true, of course. All may be paid by the organisation, but for particular meetings, such as a work's council, they may be present because they volunteered to attend.

- Commitment could be high or low:
  - low if they feel they have been forced to become a member of the group because no one else would do it;

– high if they have a particular interest or a strong sense of 'vocation' to serve in this way, or see it as an opportunity to influence how they are treated or how the organisation is run.

- Volunteers are giving of their own time and one would think they would want to use the time most effectively. This is not always the case. They may well be less focused on the business in hand because they might view the meeting as partially a social event and not just a matter of getting business carried out as effectively as possible.
- There are no real sanctions to ensure delegated tasks are carried out.
- Volunteers may be very well informed of the topic in view but sometimes they may have little or no knowledge – for example, when accounts or legal matters are being discussed.
- Their role may be seen in personal rather than 'professional' terms and there may well be uncertainty about the role itself.
- There is no guarantee that the committee is made up of the 'right' mix of people.
- The regular attendance of volunteers can be an issue.

b. Paid members

Since such meeting are part of their work, their attitude to meetings will in part be shaped by their attitude to their work and to the company/organisation.

In the end the company/organisation has sanctions – members are paid to undertake tasks allocated to them and to do so on time.

It is up to those calling the meeting to ensure that the right mix of people is present to achieve its purpose. This should be easier to achieve in a group of paid members compared to a purely volunteer group.

The social element will be less obvious – though not entirely absent. Some members may see each other infrequently and view the meeting as an opportunity to catch up with others.

c. Mixed

This presents its own strengths and weaknesses and requires sensitivity on the part of all. Paid officials can either be felt to dominate or be subservient to the volunteers.

Amy June, have you ever thought of joining the Committee? I'm sure you'd be very welcome and there's been a vacancy for ages since Bert moved away. It's only four meetings a year really – well, if you don't get put on a sub-committee. But that won't happen to start with. We sort of organise things.

June Well, I don't know. I don't know much about running things. And I'm no good with accounts and that. But I could always help with the teas. I'll think about it.

Amy I'll let Sid know you're interested then, shall I? There's a meeting sometime next month.

Becoming a member

a. By election

The most obvious body to have elected members is the House of Commons, but its size and complexity takes it outside the scope of this book. It is usually the 'management' committees of organisations that have elected members, and such organisations vary, from golf clubs to trade unions, from Parish Church Councils (PCCs) to residents' associations. Elections are expected to be democratic, open and transparent. The people elected will need to have given their agreement to be elected, although that may have been after a bit of arm twisting and lobbying.

There is normally, although not always, an agreed period of service. This can be helpful to both the person elected and the organisation.

For the individual it means there is a time limit to their commitment and they will not get 'stuck' because no one else is willing to stand. For an organisation it means there is a healthy turnover of members without the embarrassment of trying to get rid of a member whose effectiveness disappeared some time ago. Continuity can be very useful, of course, and the constitution of the organisation may well make room for re-election.

The constitution or terms of reference of the body should also make it clear whether the elected person is a **delegate** or a **representative.** The terms loosely mean the same, but their difference is most apparent when it comes to exercising the right to vote. Delegates should vote according to the will of those who elected them, while representatives use their own expertise and power to decide how to vote.

So, for example, while the majority of the electorate might want to have capital punishment, MPs may still vote against it. They are, in this sense, representatives of the people, not their delegates. Most elected members of committees, etc. are representatives, although they will be conscious of and will not ignore the views of those they represent, who in turn may wish to hold them answerable for the decisions they make. In general, however, representatives have a greater freedom to exercise their own opinions.

In order to deal with the most serious issues within the workings of the committee, most bodies have a recognised way of dismissing an elected member, including reference back to the electors and agreed reasons for a dismissal.

b. By invitation

At best this will happen when a group recognises it has need of a particular skill or expertise and seeks out someone who has this and who is willing to join the group. This is a kind of 'head hunting' and could be undertaken even where there is a subsequent election involved, helping to ensure a suitable person is nominated. Such a person may be very pleased to have been invited and brings both commitment and effectiveness.

More often, however, this is a quite informal matter and is the way a group seeks to ensure there are no vacancies. It's a matter of people knowing people and getting them to 'come along'. The informality has its strengths but can be a disadvantage if the person approached proves to be unsuitable or ineffective, especially if there are no formally agreed terms of service.

c. Ex-officio or by role

Whether the majority of members are elected or not, a group may well have members who are present purely because of the role or office they hold, such as the vicar on a PCC, the head teacher on a board of governors, the treasurer on a finance committee. Such people are usually key to the working of the group or organisation. In some situations, however, such as where a clergyperson has an ex-officio position on a trust or a board of governors, they may have no interest in the work of the particular group or simply not enough time to fulfil their membership effectively. In these circumstances, there are normally ways in which they can nominate an alternate person to take their place. This is less likely to occur where a member is present by their role within the organisation – such as secretary or safety officer – rather than because of a role outside it – for example, local parish councillor.

d. By default

No organisation or group seeks to gain members by default but the reality is, especially in voluntary organisations and groups, that there may be some members who feel that they are present merely because no one else would take it on. Metaphorically, when volunteers were asked for, everyone else took a step back, and this left them with little choice. Some such members actually prove to be very effective, but this tends to be the exception rather than the rule. Some just fill a seat at a meeting and contribute little, not really knowing why they are there and probably wishing they weren't.

Numbers

Recent government thinking on school governing bodies has led them to require such bodies to look again at their articles of management and to ensure that there are not too many people on the governing board. The principle is clear: don't just fill bodies with numbers. Make sure the number of people ensures that the work of the meeting is carried out effectively. A dozen is probably a lot better than 25.

As we will see later, effectiveness depends in part on everyone feeling they have a part to play and a contribution to make. Of course, there will be some meetings where the topic under discussion is not in a member's specific area of expertise or interest, and contributions may be more difficult on that occasion. But over a series of meetings everyone should feel they have something to contribute and be able to present their point of view. In large meetings this is less easy to do. It is also easier to 'hide' in a big meeting and to dodge any jobs that emerge from it. Committees are not at their best when they carry passengers.

It is not always possible for the chair or other officers to determine the number of members. That may be set down in the constitution, and where members are elected it may be a matter of the fair representation of a number of interested parties. But if it is felt the numbers are too large, it is always worth the committee itself looking at its constitution and seeing if there are ways to reduce the number so that the committee can be more effective.

Roles and responsibilities

An ad hoc group meeting will normally have been set up for a single purpose, and it should be reasonably clear to all attending what the purpose is.

More permanent groups will usually have a wider remit and it is important that members know not only what the terms of reference of the group are but also what the responsibilities of the members are, both corporately and individually. It is particularly important that new members are made aware of these things.

- Does the body have statutory responsibilities and powers?
- Who is the body answerable to?
- What powers does it have to appoint sub-committees or working groups?
- Are individuals financially liable for the work of the group?
- Is there any legal liability?

So, for example, a sub-committee of a main governing or management group will need to know what precisely is the purpose of the sub-committee and what powers and responsibilities it has. A trust's grant-making body will need to have a clear understanding of the terms of the trust and the criteria it operates in making grants, in order to ensure consistency and fairness as well as legal probity. Other questions a group will need to keep in mind are:

- Does the group have the power to make decisions or is it simply advisory, with only the power to make recommendations?
- If the group has the power to make decisions, are there any limits to the kind of decision it can make?
- Does the group have control over any aspects of a budget? If so, to what level?
- Do any of the members have a pecuniary or other conflict of interest in the matters under discussion by the group? If so, they should be declared.

Clarity of roles and responsibilities also gives clarity to appropriate **boundaries**, and this can help to ensure that a group does not tread on sensitive areas beyond its remit. For example, a school governing body does not have responsibility for the everyday management of the school – that is the head teacher's and senior leadership team's responsibility. It can cause unnecessary difficulties if a body whose role is strategic and monitoring begins to micro-manage.

In a meeting which involves an enquiry or a disciplinary matter, some members may be present as 'support' for the person under investigation. It is very important that the role of the supporter is well understood, especially with regard to what and how any contribution can be made.

It is also important that roles among members of a meeting are understood – a committee's secretary is not responsible for chairing the meeting, and it is not the PCC treasurer's role to decide what money shall be spent on, although of course they may very appropriately advise on the financial implications of any expenditure. In many groups, the 'officers' are there to offer advice, not to make the final decisions. This can be seen very clearly in meetings of a council where the elected members are there to make decisions but the officers are present to offer advice.

Angie If that Harry has another go at me in the meeting I'll just pack it in. Who does he think he is? It doesn't matter what I say, he always has a go at me. And what does he know about running raffles anyhow? We only sold 37 tickets the time he tried. He's so negative. Thinks he always knows best. I'm sure it's because my Jim beat him in the single's final last year. As though that's got anything to do with it.

Relationships

Personal relationships between members of the group should not affect the work of a meeting, but inevitably they do. They can make for effective meetings or for meetings that are difficult or even unpleasant. Meetings, after all, are between people, not robots.

There are relationships that only exist in the context of the meetings themselves, but most often members know at least some of the group outside the setting of the meetings, either in a social or a work context or both. Admiration, trust and friendship beyond the meeting will have a positive impact, and mistrust, dislike and grievance a negative impact. It is easy to say that the only things that matter are the purpose of the meeting, the quality of the contributions made, whoever from, and the decisions made. But in practice it is easier said than done. A good chair will be conscious of such relationships and their potential impacts and seek to take them into account while managing the meeting.

Knowledge, experience and expertise

It will be clear from what has already been said that a meeting is not effective when it is made up of people who are simply filling seats. Effectiveness comes from what the members bring to the table and the use they make of it.

The **knowledge** looked for in a member is related to the overall purpose of the group or a specific aspect of its responsibilities. So, for example, the general purpose of a PCC is the oversight of the life of the local church, its congregation and its mission, and within that it will be important that there are members who have financial knowledge, knowledge about buildings, knowledge about the needs of the local community, etc. Similarly, a school governing body that has overall strategic and monitoring responsibilities will need members who have knowledge of educational data, finances, buildings, safeguarding, admission appeals, etc.

A particular meeting may not call upon that specific knowledge, but at some point it certainly will. Any one member of the group cannot be expected to be knowledgeable at any depth on all possible matters, but within the total membership all major aspects should be covered. Total absence of such knowledge will seriously inhibit the effectiveness of the group to carry out its function.

The same is true for **experience** and **expertise**. At the most general level it is important that at least some members at a meeting have experience of the type of meeting being held and the topics being discussed. While it is helpful if new members have some relevant experience, this cannot always be guaranteed. It does, however, raise issues about the way new members are inducted into the life of the group and its meetings.

In some instances, a meeting is held where the group does not possess the expertise needed to make informed decisions on the topic under discussion. An **outside expert** or **consultant** may be brought into the meeting to fill this gap. But the group should have within it sufficient general knowledge to be able to respond to the information and to make sensible decisions as a result. A good dose of common sense will often be sufficient – but not always.

When a group is seeking to fill a vacancy, it can be very important to consider:

- the balance of knowledge and expertise within the group;
- likely future topics to be discussed and the decisions that will need to be made;
- therefore what knowledge and expertise is needed.

Ideally, a new member will be found who fills a major gap.

What this clearly indicates is the importance for both long-standing and ad hoc meetings to have a membership that holds between them the relevant skills, knowledge, experience and expertise if effective work is to be carried out. It is the membership as a whole that needs the range of knowledge and expertise. It does not all have to reside in just one individual. Indeed, the group will be less effective if it is assumed that one member does have all the knowledge – especially if this is the chair.

Personality and role

There is a tendency for us to assume that other people work in the same way we do – or if they don't, they should! Actually, it is a great blessing that people are different, work differently, learn differently, behave differently. The world would be a far less interesting place if they didn't, and most probably the clone-like humans would still be sitting in caves wondering why so little progress seemed to be made.

Various bodies have researched the subtle, complex and fascinating differences that make people who they are. Psychologists study individuals; sociologists investigate the differences in communities and societies. Work has also been done on the different kinds of people that can be found among the membership of a meeting or organisational group and the different ways they have of behaving within the group.

a. The Myers-Briggs® personality inventory

Through the use of a detailed questionnaire, a preferred choice is offered in four different areas. The choice made indicates the personality type in that aspect:

1. Do you prefer to focus on the 'world out there' or on your own inner world? This indicates 'extraversion' (E) or 'introversion' (I).
2. Do you prefer to focus on the basic information you acquire or do you prefer to add meaning and interpretation? This indicates 'sensing' (S) or 'intuition' (N).
3. When you make a decision, do you first consider the logic and consistency or first look at the people and the special circumstances involved? This indicates 'thinking' (T) or 'feeling' (F).
4. When you deal with the outside world, do you prefer to get things decided or prefer to leave things open for new information and options? This is called 'judging' (J) or 'perceiving' (P).

The choices made then give an overall four-letter 'type' – such as ESTJ. There is no 'correct' personality type, and individuals may be strongly one aspect, such as a T (thinker) as against F (feeler), or may actually be a close mix with just a preference for one aspect over another. The preferred 'type' indicates the way individuals most consistently behave and the best kind of contribution they can make. Because there is no 'right' way, it is important that differences are valued and are not a reason for conflict.

b. The 'HOTS' model

Robert Allen and Mark Victor Hanson suggest some categories into which people fall:[1]

'**H**ares'	are 'ideas' people, always coming up with new ideas.
'**O**wls'	are those who are good at analysis and can work out which are the best ideas.
'**T**urtles'	are the people who check for problems and possible mistakes. They slow down processes.
'**S**quirrels'	implement what has been decided and make things happen.

c. The Belbin® team role indicator

This was devised by Meredith Belbin as a result of his studies of various teams. Although not without its critics, it has been widely used in management training to help people working in a team situation – for example, members of a committee – to enable them to better understand the way they are working in terms of the role they fulfil. A person may adopt one role consistently or adopt differing roles in differing circumstances. In this sense, the inventory is not the same as a personality type. The nine identified roles, the contribution they can make and some drawbacks are:

1. Plant – creative and imaginative, the plant will come up with new ideas and solve difficult problems. Can ignore detail and not be good at communicating effectively.
2. Resource investigator – enthusiastic and communicative, the resource investigator builds up contacts and explores. Can be over-optimistic and lose interest after initial enthusiasm.

---

1 Mark Victor Hansen and Robert Allen, *The One Minute Millionaire* (Vermillion, 2002).

3. Coordinator – mature and confident, the coordinator identifies talent, effectively delegates and clarifies goals. Can appear to be manipulative and to be offloading own work on to others.

4. Shaper – dynamic and thrives on pressure. The shaper has courage and determination to overcome obstacles. Can be provocative and trample on people's feelings.

5. Monitor evaluator – strategic and discerning, the monitor evaluator considers all the options and makes sound judgements. Can be unnecessarily critical and lacking in drive.

6. Teamworker – cooperative and diplomatic, the teamworker listens, averts friction and is discerning. Can seek to avoid confrontation and fail to be decisive.

7. Implementer – practical and reliable, the implementer efficiently gets ideas put into practice. Can be inflexible and fail to respond to alternative possibilities.

8. Completer finisher – conscientious and painstaking, the completer finisher searches out mistakes and polishes and perfects. Can be over anxious and unwilling to delegate.

9. Specialist – single-minded and dedicated, the specialist provides skills and knowledge that are not in general supply. Can be rather narrowly focused and give too much attention to technicalities.

Even with this rather simplistic set of descriptions it will be obvious that in a group seeking to work as a team, there is no point in everyone being a plant or a completer finisher. Having lots of bright ideas may be a great stimulus for a group, but if there is no one to point out possible flaws or to put the chosen idea into practice, little will in fact get done. The committee becomes a talking shop that may be interesting but achieves little.

By definition, the effective team needs to be made up of people who cover as full a range of these roles as possible. Most people will, in fact, perform more than one role. There is not one role that is 'right'. All have their place.

- From a team leader's or a chairperson's point of view, it is therefore important to be able to identify who is carrying out which role and to use each person appropriately.
- From the individual's point of view, it is important that they know how they work best, to offer that and at the same time to value the distinctive contribution of others.

Each role will have its part to play in an effective team.

Personal agenda

Personal agendas can get in the way of effective meetings, and if they become obtrusive they can be quite difficult to manage. Any personal financial or business interest should be declared at the outset of the meeting, but other interests are not so obvious.

This can be particularly tricky if the membership includes more than one member of a family, especially if they are husband and wife. Board meetings of privately owned, family businesses may have such membership, and it is not an uncommon occurrence in church councils. The personal relationships outside the meeting may unhelpfully carry an extraneous agenda into the meeting. This can be especially difficult if it involves the chairperson and if their objectivity and impartiality is, or is perceived to be, compromised.

Some key questions

1. How do people become members?
2. At the meeting:
   a. Who can attend?
   b. Who can speak?
   c. Who can vote?
3. Is the number of members appropriate for effective meetings?
4. Are members clear about their roles and responsibilities?
5. Does the group have among its membership the necessary knowledge, skills and expertise to fulfil its responsibilities?
6. Is there trust and respect among members?
7. Are different personality types and working styles respected and used?

TWO

Organising the meeting

The secretary's diary:

Monday 2 September

Must do (meeting 18th Sept):

1. Arrange agenda with the chair today.
2. Get reports from sub-c'tees.
3. Photocopy the management accounts report.
4. Send out minutes and agenda next week.
5. Check the room is booked.
6. Check PW is happy to receive papers electronically.

The chair's diary:

Monday 2 September

Meeting 18th Sept – things to get sorted:

1. *Sort out the agenda – items:*
    - *a. new members*
    - *b. finance report*
    - *c. dates for rest of year*
    - *d. safeguarding*
    - *e. Living wage*

   and all the usual items.

2. *Speak to DW about an induction programme – constitution, past minutes, etc., having a visit.*

3. *Tell Olive to make sure there's some heat on in the room.*

4. *Fix date to see the local planning officer.*

Purpose of the meeting

A meeting will not be effective if its purpose is not clear.

I suspect, although I have not carried out a scientific survey, that the majority of those meetings that people grumble about are ineffective because no one is clear about the precise purpose of the meeting. The meeting was in the diary; we always have one this time of year; it has to happen whether there is any point to it or not.

Little wonder that such meetings leave people frustrated, exasperated and feeling that the whole thing was a waste of time.

So whose responsibility is it to elucidate the purpose of a meeting? This will, of course, depend on the nature of the meeting, but most often it is the responsibility of the chair and the secretary (or the clerk). They should be aware not only of the past in terms of past minutes and the discussions they record, but also future concerns.

What are meetings for?

- To fulfil statutory or other responsibilities.
- To provide information.
- To conduct required business – for example, to receive audited accounts, sign off the accounts and decide on actions in the light of the auditor's report.
- To determine future actions.
- To resolve a disagreement.

The purpose will shape the agenda of the meeting.

Timing and place

Meetings that are held on a regular basis usually also have a regular time and venue. Circumstances can necessitate a change to this, and if that is the case, it is important that the agenda indicates very clearly where and when the meeting will be held on this occasion. This is the case also for irregular or one-off meetings. Reminder emails or telephone calls may help to ensure that all members are present.

When the membership changes, it is helpful if the chair ensures that the usual meeting time is convenient for all members. Where members are volunteers, such things as the day job, childcare and regular commitments can mean that certain days of the week or times of the day would preclude a person's attendance. While it may be difficult to take everyone's circumstances into account for every meeting, availability should not simply be assumed. Similar considerations should also be given with regard to the venue, especially if members come from a widely scattered area. It isn't only the chair's convenience that has to be taken into account.

Agenda

There really is no excuse for not circulating the agenda prior to the meeting. Sadly, too many meetings begin with an apology that no papers have been sent out. All sorts of excuses are offered: lack of time, miscommunication with the secretary, they weren't really necessary, etc. It is not good enough. Members have the right to know what is to be the subject of the meeting, and that is what an agenda indicates.

The most frequent complaint about agendas is that they are too full. Too many items. The solution seems to be obvious and is usually agreed by all concerned: shorter agendas but more meetings to cover the business. Too often, though, it doesn't work. We want shorter agendas but not more meetings. How are we to square the circle?

First question: Are all the items on the agenda actually necessary?

Second question: Do they have to take up so much time?

Some items appear on almost all agendas:

Welcome and apologies. In some groups, apologies have to be formally accepted. Frequent consecutive absences that have not been agreed can be a reason for resignation.

Minutes or record of the last meeting. These normally have to be agreed for accuracy and signed by the chair. This means they may then be made public.

Matters arising from the minutes that are not already itemised on the agenda.

Any other business (AOB) is a usual item at the end of the meeting. Some groups have an earlier item in which any matters to be raised at the end of the meeting are identified as an indicator of the time they may need. Other issues around AOB are dealt with below.

For ongoing groups, **the date of the next meeting** is either arranged or confirmed.

The rest of the agenda is dictated by the business to be undertaken. The chair or convener of the meeting normally has the responsibility to arrange what is included on the agenda. A selection of possible items usually has to be made and such a selection will reflect:

- the perceived urgency of the item;
- the place it has in the effective working of the group or organisation;
- the concerns of members.

Simply including anything and everything that could be discussed will not make for an effective meeting.

To help the management of the meeting, items may have a time indicator beside them. Where this system is used there has to be some flexibility, but it does at least give members an idea of how the meeting will go. Items may also have a name against them indicating who is responsible for introducing that topic – for example, a report, the financial statement, future social activities, an appointment procedure, pupil progress data.

Papers

Many meetings have items that require accompanying papers to provide necessary information for the members. Some of these can be lengthy and quite complicated, such as accounts, tenders for contracts, pupil progress data. Members are rightly annoyed if such papers are tabled rather than circulated prior to the meeting. Time is unnecessarily wasted if it is suggested that members read the tabled papers during the meeting. Almost inevitably, such a reading will be somewhat cursory. Discussion and decisions will be less effective than would be the case if members have had an opportunity prior to the meeting to read the papers carefully and identify points of particular interest or concern.

All this seems obvious, but papers are tabled at far too many meetings. The occasions when a tabled paper can be justified are few and far between. It is normally the responsibility of the secretary or clerk of the meeting to ensure that the papers are circulated in good time, and some organisations stipulate timelines for the circulation of papers prior to a meeting. But if that is the officer's responsibility, it is the responsibility of the members to give the papers proper attention prior to the meeting. In busy lives this may mean on the train on the day of the meeting, and at least they will then be read. This is not ideal, however, as the papers could raise questions that might need to be investigated prior to the meeting. In the real world, even effective meetings have to cope with less than the ideal.

Minutes

The recording of minutes is a particular skill and in some organisations there will be an independent minute taker, i.e. an 'officer' of the meeting who is not a contributing or voting member. In less formal groups, minutes will often be taken by a member who may also be the secretary. Trying to take minutes and contribute is not easy, and attempting to chair a meeting while also recording is not to be recommended.

In Quaker (Friends) meetings, the role of both chair and minute-taker is in the hands of the clerk. In the main, however, the clerk is not expected to contribute to the discussion. They are responsible for the process of the meeting and for producing draft minutes during the course of the meeting. The meeting's acceptance of the minute(s) is made there and then. This ensures that the meeting agrees with what is recorded since at the next meeting the same members may not be present and so they would be unable to make a proper decision regarding the accuracy of the minutes. This distinctive practice among Quakers is not generally common in the world of meetings, although occasionally a meeting may decide it wishes to have a particularly significant matter minuted there and then. More usually, minutes are written up after the meeting and presented as a draft to the next meeting of the group.

A decision has to be made between the extremes of attempting to record every point voiced and simply setting down the decisions made and actions agreed. It is important, however, that the decisions and actions are accurately recorded. Minute-takers should ensure that they are clear about what has been decided or agreed. These decisions and actions will sometimes appear in bold in the written minutes. It is also useful for future reference if the minutes indicate the person responsible for the actions – for example, obtaining quotes, following up contacts, issuing service schedules, inviting a future speaker.

The important thing about minutes is that they record the things that will need to be referred to in the future and do so with as little ambiguity as possible so that there is no confusion or dispute about their meaning and that some indication is given to the range of views around a decision. It is said that Ofsted inspectors look for certain key indicators in the minutes of governors' meetings to show that governors are being rigorous in their challenge to the school leadership. So it is important that words such as asked, questioned, investigated and challenged are included and that such questions and challenges are recorded in some detail.

Video and telephone conferencing

Telephones and video links are increasingly being used in the business world for conference meetings. For global businesses they are inevitable now that the technology is available. Availability and effectiveness are, however, two different things. The technology is all too often less than perfect. Links fail or are only intermittent, resulting in frustration and interrupted meetings. Members may not even be using the same computers or software, which means that sharing data can be problematic.

Setting up such meetings needs particular care. The technology has to be managed, and this includes having someone to operate the camera for video conferencing. It should be straightforward, but in practice it seldom is. Members may have the camera aimed at the wrong level so that while eyes and hair are visible, mouths aren't. Or maybe all that can be seen is a person's chest and chin. When meetings go on for several hours, the camera operator can become bored and the screen will suddenly switch from the members to a spider in the corner of the ceiling or a ladybird crawling up the water jug.

At least with video conferencing, the presence of members who should be there can be checked. It can be even more hit and miss with telephone conferencing:

- Members should log in but might forget to do so.
- Background noise can make it difficult to hear what contributing members are saying. Members may have failed to find a quiet place in which to participate in the meeting.
- Sometimes members put their phone on mute, which certainly inhibits communication!
- There is no guarantee that someone who hasn't spoken recently is still in fact on line. There can always be a reason for leaving without informing the others, and the absence may go unnoticed by the others.

Not being able to see speakers has disadvantages and can take some getting used to. It is certainly more difficult to 'control' such meetings, especially if the discussion gets lively. It is necessary therefore to set out from the start some form of agreed procedure for how the meeting will be conducted.

There is no doubt that this technology enables meetings to be held without the time, cost and disruption of bringing all members together physically. They are ideal for short, regular meetings to track progress on already agreed courses of action. However, for occasions when detailed and difficult discussions are likely to take place, they are a poor substitute for face-to-face meetings, and they often make the already challenging job of chairing such meetings much more difficult.

Some key questions

1. Is the purpose of the meeting clear?
2. Are the time and venue of the meeting convenient for members?
3. Do meetings begin and end promptly?
4. Are agendas manageable?
5. Are agendas and papers sent out in good time?
6. Are minutes accurate, and do they record decisions and actions clearly?
7. Are video and/or telephone conferences well managed and technically effective?

THREE

Running the meeting

Who runs the meeting?

No matter how informal a meeting is, there will be some process or person who actually runs it – or seeks to ensure it runs well. Even if the meeting is ostensibly just a social gathering, in reality there is almost always some organising to be done – someone sorts out the orders for drinks, organises the seating, makes sure everyone can get home. This may not be the same person all the time – the role may move among those present. Whatever the common saying may suggest, even a 'piss-up' in a brewery needs some level of organising!

The majority of meetings, however, and the ones being focused on here, are more formal, and there is usually a designated or at least a recognised person whose role it is, sometimes just for that occasion, to run the meeting. In practice, the designated person may have the formal role of the chair, yet they may not be the one who is actually running the meeting. Weak chairpersons leave a kind of vacuum that someone will seek to fill. The meeting may be happy to go along with that if the business is being done in spite of the lack of guidance from the chair. But where there is no implicit agreement about that, there is the danger that rivalries will produce a vying for control, and the meeting is likely to become an arena for power struggles, big or small. Effectiveness is not a likely outcome!

People who are designated to run meetings may have various titles: prime minister, leader of the Council, chief executive, vicar, chair, clerk. The title itself doesn't matter; it's the role that counts. For purposes of clarity we will use the term 'chair' here.

The chair normally opens and closes the meeting, welcomes members and ensures that the agenda items are dealt with. As we noted above, it is usually the chair, in conjunction with the secretary, who arranges the agenda and is responsible for ensuring that the meeting gets through the agenda in reasonable time and with an appropriate balance of discussion for each item. It will be up to the chair to ensure that all have the opportunity to speak and no one person dominates the discussion – and especially not the chair him/herself. If a vote is required, the chair needs to conduct that clearly and efficiently.

The purpose of the meeting

Many meetings are 'repeats' – i.e. they are ongoing meetings of a committee or such like where there is a known reason for the meeting. At its broadest, this may be running the organisation or some aspect of it – for example, a health and safety meeting, a finance meeting, a summer fayre meeting. People will have a reasonably clear idea what the meeting will be about, at least in general terms, and the agenda will give the details.

But where a meeting is a one-off or the first of a short-term series of meetings, it is important that everyone is quite clear at the outset about the purpose of the meeting. The chair (or meeting convenor) should set this out and ensure that everyone present understands the purpose. Without such clarity, discussion will inevitably be diffused and members will feel confused and frustrated.

Even where the general purpose of the meeting is understood, the agenda may include items that are novel or out of the ordinary. Accompanying papers may have helped, but the purpose of that particular item may need to be clarified.

Clarification of the purpose should not merely set out the topic of the meeting or item but also indicate whether the item is for information, for discussion only, or requires a recommendation to be made or a decision to be taken.

Timing

Some chairs like to have an indicative timing set against each item of the agenda. This provides a guideline on the pacing of the meeting and indicates the chair's estimate of the relative importance or complexity of items. In the light of actual discussion there will need to be some flexibility in applying this, but if such a 'timetable' is regularly ignored, it would be better not to have it put on the agenda.

Whether timings are given in detail or not, the chair should indicate at the outset the expected length of the meeting. Some flexibility will be needed, but frequent and excessive overrunning should be avoided. Meetings that are overlong (especially if there is no break) or that frequently overrun are not efficient and cause annoyance. On the other hand, an arbitrary closure of an item that is insensitive to the actual discussion should also be avoided.

Contributions and discussion

Members look to the chair to have control of the meeting. Without such control, members can become anxious or confused and feel that the meeting lacks direction. They would be right. Control does not mean everything is so buttoned up that there is no real opportunity for discussion. That would make the members feel they are merely being treated as rubber stamps and that their contribution and views are pointless.

Control means that at worst the meeting does not descend to chaos or a shouting match and at best offers a structured way for the business to be conducted, for members to contribute and be listened to, and for decisions to be made where that is required. The skilful chair will achieve this without it being overly apparent.

Enabling all members to make the contribution they wish to without anyone dominating the proceedings means that the chair needs to listen carefully not only to the individual contributions but also to the flow of the whole discussion. It requires good judgement as to when to allow discussion to be extended because new points are still being made and when to draw the discussion to a conclusion because there is a danger of points merely being repeated.

When all members are contributing and their points are both helpful and reasonably concise, the chair's job is relatively easy. It is not so easy if points are irrelevant, overly long or repetitive. Sensitive firmness is required. Merely slapping a member down either for their viewpoint or for the length of their contribution makes for neither a happy nor an effective meeting.

Contributions should be welcomed, listened to and allowed to take their place in the overall discussion. Members should treat one another with appropriate respect, and if necessary the chair should remind the meeting of this if the discussion gets overheated.

Effective membership will normally mean that present at the meeting are people with distinctive contributions to make, varied expertise and experience and a desire to ensure that decisions are good and well grounded. Members will bring different perspectives to the discussion, and it is not only the 'expert' in any particular field who has a valuable contribution to make. The person with the least knowledge may be the one who asks the most pertinent question or shows the most common sense.

The better a chair knows and understands the members, the easier it is. Individual styles will be known – those whose contribution is only made after encouragement, those who are too loquacious, those who are always worth hearing but who often leave their contribution to near the end of the discussion, those who always start with a negative. Knowing the team means the chair can draw the best out of each member and help to ensure the meeting works well *together*.

This, of course, assumes that everyone present is actually wanting to work together and to produce positive outcomes in an effective way.

But that may not always be the case. Individuals can be obstructive. There can be underlying power struggles. Hidden agendas may be at work. The actual contribution and discussion may be driven by hidden motives, and to control this may be tricky.

In some meetings, the process for speaking can be very formal. All contributions and discussion is 'through' the chair and members only speak when invited. This is true, for example, in a Quaker meeting where members indicate their wish to contribute (to 'minister') and are called to do so by the clerk. It is a measured way of proceeding and ensures that each contribution is listened to without interruption. Such a process becomes part of the accepted culture of a meeting, and members are expected to comply with that culture, whatever it is. So long as there is respect among members, there are opportunities for making a contribution and all contributions are listened to, there is no one right process – only the right one for that particular group.

Disagreement

Effective meetings are not necessarily those in which everyone agrees with one another (apart, of course, from the congenital 'nit-picker' who never lets anything go past without a complaint). In fact, meetings in which there is no difference of opinion could be inefficient and lacking serious attention to the issues at hand. The more significant the agenda item, the more likely there is to be disagreement. And a strong membership team will add to this likelihood.

Disagreement is not the same as dysfunction. What matters is how the disagreement is handled and how it is resolved. Strong arguments need to be heard *and listened to* and it is important that everyone, especially the chair, weighs the arguments put forward. Ideally the arguments should be put without it becoming a personal contest between individuals or groups of members. Strong opinions can be accompanied by strong feelings, and while feelings cannot be ignored, they should not be allowed to dominate discussion.

Passion can be important, but if it becomes deaf to any and every counterproposal, it can be obstructive and simply appear like 'a bee in the bonnet' which can then be 'swatted' out of the way.

Opinion Difference Disagreement
Argument Aggression Abuse

In business meetings of employees there are implicit sanctions against the disagreement descending into personal attack (although it is known to happen). This is less obvious when the meeting is of volunteers, and the chair will need to be very firm to ensure argument does not become abuse. At best, the culture of a meeting will allow disagreement within a sensibly controlled process.

There may be occasions when the disagreement is so fierce that the chair will need to call 'time out' to allow tempers to cool and to give time for reflection. This is all part of the management of the meeting and of any conflict that might arise. While it is not always possible, it is important to attempt to keep the disagreement within the bounds of the meeting. Ongoing wrangles in the corridor, the toilets or in the car park after the meeting seldom produce better long-term outcomes and generally become increasingly personalised.

Decision

At some point, the discussion, whether there has been a disagreement or not, will need to be brought to a conclusion. Occasionally this will mean a vote – either because that is required by the process or because it is felt that a record of how people have felt is important.

The chair, or the secretary, should remind members of the formal procedure for voting – whether this is by secret paper voting or by a show of hands, and the process in the case of a tied vote. It is important in meetings where non-members are present that it is made clear who has the right to vote.

It is then vital that the chair makes it crystal clear what the vote is on. It is surprising how many times a meeting is called to vote on a subject only for members to look at one another and indicate that they are not sure what exactly the vote is on.

Votes should indicate those who are for the motion, those against and those who abstain. A record of the voting figures needs to be kept.

VOTE

1. Is the matter to be voted on clear?
2. Who can vote?
3. How will the vote be taken?
4. What's the outcome?

Voting is not the only way for a meeting to indicate its decisions. Most often it is a matter of clear agreement and no vote is necessary, or indeed felt to be desirable. Voting can sometimes be felt to be a divisive process that only hardens opinion and breaks a sense of the group working together. Quakers, for example, never take a vote, and in fact do not even see the decision arrived at as a matter of consensus. They would see it as a matter of the meeting discerning what is already the will of God, having been guided by the Holy Spirit. The clerk prepares a minute of the discussion during the course of the meeting itself and the meeting is then invited to agree that minute, with amendments made as necessary.

Consensus means that the meeting as a whole, but not necessarily unanimously as individuals, agrees to a proposed recommendation, decision or course of action.

It is quite possible for members to disagree with a decision as individuals while agreeing that it should be taken by the meeting as a whole. An individual may even wish for their minority view to be recorded in the minutes. What is important in such circumstances, however, is that everyone understands that the corporate decision of the meeting is what counts and is what all members outside the meeting stand by. It can be very destructive if the dissenting voice is taken out of the meeting and is heard telling reporters, parents in the playground, parishioners at the back of the church, playing partners on the golf course, that they disagreed with the decision and then seek to undermine it.

Edgar You're just going to have to have a word with Alec.

Gerald What's he been up to this time?

Edgar You know we agreed to divide the charity giving in two this year – one to a local charity and another overseas.

Gerald Only he didn't agree, did he? I thought he'd never let it go – his thing about 'charity begins at home'. I could see he wasn't happy with the way the vote went.

Edgar Well, he's now been telling all his cronies that it's not his fault their money is going to Africa. Told them straight he was against it. Why can't he just stand by the decision of the meeting like he should? Everyone else does – even Peggy, and I know she disagreed with it. But you don't hear her going round sucking up to people, telling them she was against it.

The outcome of a vote or decision, however it is arrived at, needs to be clearly recorded. Too often disagreements about minutes revolve not around what was discussed, but around the actual decision reached. It is vital that the secretary is very clear about the decision and if there is uncertainty that they request clarity before the meeting moves on to the next item of the agenda.

Decisions and recommendations require someone to take action. Some of these may clearly be the responsibility of the secretary: policy papers requested for the next meeting, the room to be booked for an extra meeting, a letter of thanks to be sent to a recent speaker. Some may be undertaken by the chair. Other actions or tasks may be delegated to particular members: these should be made clear at the meeting and noted in the minutes.

Ending the meeting

Most agendas have a set number of items at the end just as they do at the beginning. These would normally include any other business and date of next meeting.

Any other business (AOB) can be problematic if left as a free for all. Just as everyone is looking forward to the end of the meeting and beginning to gather their papers together, someone raises an issue out of the blue that no one had seen coming but everyone recognises is important and cannot just be left. It throws the whole timing of a meeting out, annoys those who need to get away and usually manages to wrong-foot the chair. It should not happen but it does.

There are a number of ways this can be prevented.

- Members are requested at the time of the sending out of the agenda to let the chair or secretary know of any item they would wish to bring up under AOB.
- It is made clear that any items not indicated to the chair or secretary prior to the meeting will not be dealt with at that meeting but will be put on the agenda of the following meeting.
- An agenda item towards the beginning of the meeting provides members the opportunity to indicate any AOB item they wish to raise. This is noted and it provides the chair with warning about the timing of the whole agenda.

No doubt there are exceptional occasions when an important matter does arise at the last minute, but there is no reason why the chair should not be informed immediately before the meeting. If the matter is being raised by the chair, they should mention it at the outset of the meeting.

It is normal for members to be reminded of the date of the next meeting or, where this has not already been fixed, to make that arrangement. Most groups that meet regularly will normally fix meetings anything up to a year ahead.

The chair should thank members (and officers present) for their attendance and their contributions and then formally close the meeting. Minutes normally indicate what time the meeting closes.

Enjoyment

An effective, well-run meeting at which members have felt they have had the opportunity to contribute, the group has worked well together and positive decisions have been made, and all in good time, should be an enjoyable experience. Meetings are not meant to be boring, a waste of time, an arena for antagonism. Enjoyment is important in an effective meeting.

In some organisations, ice-breaker exercises are used at the beginning of a meeting, especially where the members have not previously known each other. Some people find this very helpful and it can help to ensure the group works well together. For others, such exercises are anathema and they only increase a sense of awkwardness. Social contact outside the working of the group, such as members meeting for a meal or just having a drink together, can sometimes prove helpful.

Jennifer I thought that went rather well, didn't you? Much better now that Oliver is chair. He really gets things moving.

Mark Much more focused than Stephen used to be – but then what can you expect. He must have been knocking on 75!

Jennifer I like the way we have things timed now. And since he chased Sylvia up we do get the papers before the meeting. I think he's going to be very good.

Mark Yes, he's OK – and gives everyone a chance to have their say without it going on for ever.

Jennifer It was news to me that we could be having a new clubhouse, but I suppose that's the kind of thing he has to think about.

Mark Absolutely. Must dash. See you next month.

Some key questions

1. Does the chair run the meeting effectively?
2. Does the chair clarify the purpose of the meeting and items on the agenda as necessary?
3. Does the chair give items appropriate time?
4. Does the chair keep the meeting to time?
5. Do all members have the opportunity to contribute?
6. How well does the chair know individual members and their knowledge, skills and expertise?
7. Do all members show each other respect?

8. Are differing views handled positively?
9. Are decisions clearly indicated and minuted?
10. Are voting procedures correctly followed?
11. Do people know who are expected to carry out delegated tasks?
12. Was the meeting enjoyable?

FOUR

Leadership

The role of the chair at a meeting is vital for the effective and efficient running of the meeting. This should be clear from all that has already been said. The skills required to be an effective chair are similar to those exercised in other areas of leadership, not least in the leadership of teams.

There are a number of **key factors**:

1. Ensuring the membership of a body know each other and what areas of expertise or knowledge they have, as well as their roles. This is important when creating a new body or where new members are introduced to an existing body.

2. Understanding both the scope and the limits of the role. It is not the task of the chair to do everything – neither within the meeting nor within the wider organisation. Others have their responsibilities – the secretary, treasurer, minute-taker, clerk, principal, minister and so on. Knowing the boundaries of the role is important if the chair is not to encroach inappropriately on other people's areas of responsibility. In a school, for example, it is not the chair's role to manage the school's day-to-day working. There may be an important monitoring role, but that is different. Relationships between chairs of governors and

head teachers can be sadly undermined if this distinction and the proper boundaries are not maintained.

3. Self-awareness. In the pastoral situation, personal self-awareness is one of the most important 'tools' and a *sine qua non.* The same is true for leadership. It means self-knowledge about such things as:

   - Personal strengths – gifts, experience, expertise, skills. If you don't have a realistic awareness of your strengths you will not be able to exercise them effectively and make the contribution you should. Hiding them away under a bushel will do no one any good.
   - Personal weaknesses or vulnerabilities, including lack of knowledge on particular subjects, similarly for experience and expertise; personality style such as shyness, quick temper, defensiveness, being emotional or being too detached. The leader should not constantly apologise for such things but must be aware of them, seek to keep them in check and ensure that personal weaknesses are compensated for in the total make-up of the membership

4. Leadership. Being a chair is a leadership role. Its scope will, of course, vary depending on the nature of the meeting, whether it is a board of directors, county council, church meeting, board of governors, grants committee of a trust, a social committee, etc. But to a greater or lesser extent, leadership involves:

   - Providing direction – this may mean changing the way the whole organisation works, or simply proposing dates for the next six social activities.

- Making a difference – using one's influence to bring about changes: in the working of the committee, its programme, differences in the way the organisation is structured, where funds should be distributed.
- Working with others to achieve agreed goals – leadership is not normally a dictatorship, so it means being a team leader, encouraging, enabling and motivating others to achieve results.

5. Leadership style. Effective leaders do not all exhibit the same style. Consider Winston Churchill and Mother Teresa, Lord Nelson and Nelson Mandela. Different contexts call for different styles. No one style is effective in all circumstances. Different styles might include:

    - Coercive – 'I'm telling you, you must do it now.'
    - Authoritative – 'This is the direction we should take, and this is why.'
    - Affiliative – 'We've got to pull together on this.'
    - Consultative – 'I'd like to hear your views on this.'
    - Pace-setting – 'This is the way it should be done and by this date.'

Individuals will have their preferred style, but good leaders know when to modify that and to adopt a different one even within the context of a single meeting. So, for example, it may be important on a particular agenda item that all members are given a chance to air their views and make their contribution – so a 'consultative' style is adopted. But if the discussion is rambling on, there may come a point at which the chair calls the discussion to an end and decides that a decision now has to be made. This is a more coercive style. Each style has its strengths and its weaknesses.

STYLE	STRENGTHS	WEAKNESSES
COERCIVE	Decisive	Can be resented
AUTHORITATIVE	Can be justified, based on knowledge	Can undermine contribution of others
AFFILIATIVE	Creates good team spirit	Too cosy, even collusive
CONSULTATIVE	All feel involved, builds commitment	Can take a lot of time
PACE SETTER	Keeps things moving	Fails to see and explore problems

Expectations

While the chair may not be an expert on every item that arises in an agenda, it is expected that they will have a good understanding of the purposes of the particular meeting. Where that meeting is a major committee or governance group of the total organisation, the chair will also be expected to have a good general knowledge of the wider context within which the organisation operates: general market conditions, national educational policy and legislation, national church priorities, etc.

As leader of the group, the chair can be expected to:

- enable members to understand the vision and the ethos that inform all that the meeting does;
- identify issues;
- be aware of problems;
- identify support that the group may need;
- ensure there is effective communication within the group and to others beyond it;

- prioritise;
- know any constitutional or statutory requirements.

Clearly, the level at which these occur will very much depend on the nature of the group itself and its role within an organisation – the meeting of the Sunday school teachers will not have the same concerns as the Parish Church Council; the health and safety committee will not have the same issues to handle as the board of directors, and that will affect the demands made on the chair.

Leadership may, of course, be the role of the whole meeting group and not just the responsibility of the chair within the group. So a board of directors, a board of governors, a Parochial Church Council will have a leadership role within the life of the company, the school, the parish. Under the leadership of the chair, the meeting membership will be expected to provide:

- vision;
- direction;
- strategy;
- understanding and management of change;
- the building of relationships within and beyond the organisation;
- coherence between actions taken and principles held.

All these will help shape the agendas of the meetings.

Some key questions

1. Does the chair know the scope and limits of the role?
2. Is the chair self-aware?
3. Does the chair fulfil the appropriate leadership role?
4. Is the chair aware of their own preferred leadership style and able to change it as appropriate?
5. Does the chair fulfil appropriate expectations?
6. Enabled by the chair, does the group exercise its appropriate leadership role?

FIVE

Change

It's an old joke:

Question	How many vicars does it take to change a light bulb?
Answer	What do you mean, 'change'?

This is a bit unfair on vicars – and in any case they certainly aren't the only ones who find change difficult. Most people find it much easier to continue doing what they always have, in the way they always have. Even those who are excited by change usually find it easier if they are the ones who initiate the change rather than have it imposed on them. But changing circumstances require changed processes, new markets, a different curriculum, a revised schedule of services. The more one is committed to the current product range, the way maths is taught, the time of Matins, holding meetings only on Wednesdays, the more difficult it will feel to make any changes.

Constant change is unsettling for everyone and can lead to a drop in morale. One only has to think of the impact of constant change on the NHS or schools. But for most organisations, standing still actually means slipping back, so change is important – just so long as it is perceived to be for the better and can be sensibly justified. Change for change's sake isn't helpful.

In a society where change is constant and rapid, as in the West at the moment, people look to certain institutions to provide a sense of stability. For some, that is the royal family, for others their local bridge club, and for others their church. They are by nature conservative institutions and have a social role by being so. And for that reason, any change in these institutions can be even more difficult for some people to face.

Meetings, especially those where strategic decisions have to be made, will properly and inevitably have to handle change. Indeed, it is their role to consider and initiate change. That doesn't mean, however, that every member is going to feel happy about it, and there will be some who by inclination or viewpoint will resist a particular proposal for change.

The members of a main committee will need to take into account the prevailing attitudes towards change that exist within their organisation – not because they will determine whether or not a change should happen, but because they could have an impact on the process of implementing the changes, how resistance may be overcome, the timescales involved, the cost implications, etc. This will be complex for a major change such as a local education authority changing from a three- to a two-tier schooling system, or a large manufacturing company relocating its headquarters and main factory. But the principles are no different in a smaller organisation where the changes are less far reaching but nevertheless can raise anxiety and resistance.

The change curve

Management trainers have various ways of showing the responses that people make to a proposed change. The Kubler-Ross change curve, produced in the 1960s out of research into how patients respond to the news of having cancer, is perhaps the best known, and many variations have been produced since. The curve indicates the process over a period of time. At its simplest it may include:

Shock:
The news of the change may be 'a bolt from the blue' and initially cause shock. There is fear of the unknown. There may be inadequate information. There is the tendency to keep looking back.

- I never thought things were as bad as that.
- What do you mean, he resigned?!
- How can we possibly be in the red?
- It was all right the way it was.

Denial:
On hearing that a change is proposed, there is a denial of any need for the change and statement that in fact it will not happen.

- It won't work here!
- We've tried it before and it didn't work then.
- There's no need for it.
- Why are we having to change?

Anger:
The fact is that there is going to be change, and that makes the person feel angry.

- It's always us who have to change.
- They don't care how we feel.
- I'll show them! We'll put a stop to it.

Anger may give way to a sense of apathy or a feeling of depression when activity, morale and productivity are at their lowest.

Exploration:
Realising that the change is not going to go away, most people will seek ways of making it possible for them to live with it, and they look for a

favourable outcome. The viewpoint becomes more forward looking and even hopeful.

- What if we do this?
- Couldn't we go about it like this?
- I'd be happier if . . .

Acceptance:
The person has understood the need for the change, has found a way to live with it and has come to accept it as a way forward.

- I reckon I could manage to live with that.
- That's the way we should go.
- I think it will actually be better like that.

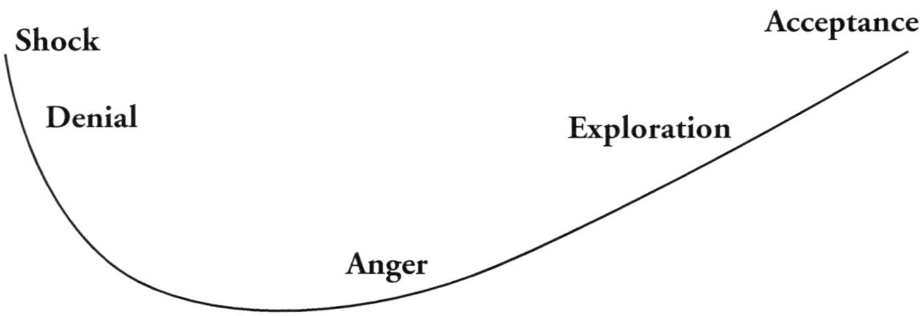

Individuals will react differently: some move through the curve quickly, even missing some elements; others will move more slowly and even get stuck.

When an organisation is going through change, this process will be reflected in the responses of the people in the organisation as a whole, be it a company going through restructuring, a school becoming an academy, a parish being amalgamated with another. But the same processes will also happen when small groups of people, such as committees, are faced with change and the need to make changes.

It is important for the chair to identify as far as is possible how each individual is reacting and to help them through the process. This may mean going through the information and reasons with individuals, giving reassurance about a person's own position in the light of the change, and/or helping the person to see the wider vision that lies behind the change.

Acceptance of change

Getting change to be accepted isn't a matter of luck or simply a question of the passing of time. There are certain things that can help the process:

- Communication. Keep people informed. Anxieties rise if information is partial or absent. A vacuum of information means people will fill it with their guesses, fantasies and fears. Conspiracies will be seen where there are none.
- Clarity. Be clear what the change is, the reason for it and, in so far as this can be known, the implications both for individuals and the organisation.
- Give good reasons for the change and a vision of what the change will achieve.
- Have a plan for how to achieve the change:

REASON + VISION + PLAN = CHANGE

- Reason and a plan without vision will lead to confusion.
- Vision and a plan with no reason for the change will lead to resistance.
- Reason and vision but with no plan to implement it will just produce anxiety and achieve little.

While the process will require a rational approach, on its own that will not be enough. Indeed, before change can be accepted there will be other barriers to overcome, including **emotional** ones. We have seen that proposed change can lead to anxiety, fear, anger and depression. There will therefore need to be enthusiasm, reassurance, an understanding of people's needs and clarity about the roles people will have, enabling engagement in the process and an encouragement to move forward.

On the wider scene, there will be '**political**' issues: the building-up of support, the engagement of the wider community/organisation, gaining support of stakeholders, such as parents, trade unions, the deanery.

In the abstract, this may feel a long way from what goes on in the meetings you know. But in practice, in any meeting where change is the issue, these processes will be involved to a greater or lesser extent. And it will be largely up to the chair to be aware of what is going on and to manage the process.

Kevin So what did you think of that, then? As far as I can see it's totally unnecessary. If it ain't broke, don't change it, is what I say. And we're doing OK.

Gary But that's the trouble – we aren't. Carry on the way we are and there'll be nothing left for us to run. I think he had a point. He made good sense to me.

Kevin That's all right for you to say. It won't affect you like it will me. You don't live round here. He didn't say anything that convinced me.

Gary Well, I think it could have a lot of support once people know what it's all about and the reasons behind it. I think we should give it a try.

Some key questions

1. Is the group willing and able to initiate and manage appropriate change?
2. Is the group aware of the change curve and its implications?
3. Is the group enabled to move from shock to acceptance in the face of change?
4. Does the group have a reason, a vision and a plan for proposed changes?

SIX

After the meeting's over

When a meeting has gone badly, all you want to do is get out and get home. But good or bad, a meeting isn't the end of the matter. There are still things to be done.

Conscientious and committed members don't simply leave the meeting and forget all about it. In one way or another they reflect on what happened. It may be for only a few minutes just summing up for themselves how it felt, how they did. But more detailed reflection is also likely – not least by the chair. Good chairs and members are, in fact, 'reflective practitioners' – they think about their contribution and consider what might have been better, what shouldn't have been done or said, what was omitted that should have been said or done.

What was achieved?

Was it a really productive meeting? Were members really engaged and contributing? Were there clear decisions and a good consensus? Did it go well and feel quite enjoyable? Was it a worthwhile experience?

OR

Was it a right waste of time and effort? A lot of talk and nothing decided? Was it dominated by a few and no one else given a chance? Frustrating and annoying? Too much heat and not enough light?

What made the good experience; what made the bad experience? These things don't happen by accident. Unless someone thinks about it, the good could go sour and the bad get worse.

Decisions

Some decisions, like the acceptance of a report or signing off the accounts, are completed at the meeting, but most decisions have ramifications beyond the meeting itself. Actions will be decided on that will have to be taken further. Recommendations to other bodies will need to be communicated. Invitations to speakers will have to be sent, the acceptance of the tender conveyed to the builder. Who will do each of these should have been made clear at the meeting when the decision was taken. Leaving it all to the secretary or chair by default is not good enough. Some actions could be better undertaken by a member, and for members to have actions to carry out between meetings can increase a sense of commitment and involvement.

Monitoring

It would be good to think that everyone is entirely responsible, will always do what they said they would and that no one ever forgets things. But the world isn't like that, and with the best will in the world, actions decided at meetings can be forgotten, put off, left undone. There's that terrible feeling when the minutes arrive and you find your name against one of the action points and you had forgotten all about it. It usually means a lot of scurrying around at the last minute.

The group itself should monitor actions agreed at the last meeting or previously, and check what progress has been made or what has hindered progress. This will usually come up in the matters arising item on the agenda, but some decisions may have been taken some time ago and members lost sight of them. It is part of the chair's responsibility to keep a monitoring eye on decisions, reminding individuals where nothing seems to have happened, checking that past decisions have not been lost.

Minutes

We have already seen the importance of the minutes. It is usually the secretary's responsibility to produce draft minutes for the chair to check. It is helpful if decisions and action points are clearly set out in the text – not hidden away in a paragraph of discussion – and the person's name or initials set alongside what they have agreed to do.

Where minutes are normally made public, matters that were declared to be of a confidential nature at the meeting should be separately minuted, clearly indicated as being confidential and ideally printed on paper of a different colour. Care should be taken when distributing minutes that the confidential minutes only go to the appropriate people.

Signed copies of the minutes should be kept in their own file together with any papers that were circulated or tabled at the meeting.

Paul So that's that, then. All over till next time. I must make a note about following up on the publicity notices. I'm sure to forget otherwise. Can you remember who the printer was that Sean mentioned?

Gemma I think it was Bennett's but you'll have to check. I might suggest to Dawn that we have coffee before the meeting next time. I could always bring a few biscuits. Put everyone in a good mood!

Paul Good idea. See you. Take care.

Some key questions

1. What did the meeting achieve?
2. Were members clear about decisions taken and actions to be carried out, and by whom?
3. Are past decisions and action plans monitored?
4. Are minutes kept secure?
5. Are confidential minutes clearly indicated as such and kept confidential?

Conclusion

Meetings don't have to be boring or annoying or feel like a waste of time. With a bit of planning, careful preparation, distribution of papers well beforehand and decent chairing, they can be productive and enable everyone to feel that they have contributed. With trust among the members, a light but firm touch from the chair and a dash of humour all round, they can even be fun. You might even look forward to another meeting!